Gun T
Offensive Line Drill Book

Copyright © 2022 by Kenny Simpson and Bo Gould

All rights reserved.

ISBN:9798372092044

fbcoachsimpson.com

Reviews

"Coach Simpson's Gun T Offensive Overview is an excellent offensive resource. This course provides the foundation of Coach Simpson's offensive philosophy. Coach believes in the monikers that "Less is More" and the "Rule of 3", and both were evident in the explanation of the offense. His explanations were clear and concise, and the presentations were easy to follow."
Todd Knipp

"This is absolutely amazing. Coach Simpson does an excellent job of explaining his system. Whether you're a young coach or an experienced coach this is must see. You can easily see why he is a successful coach. His detailed organization is on point and I cannot wait to learn more from Coach Simpson."
Mike Kloes

"I've been following coach Simpson for a while now and it's very clear to me that even though I may not be a HC, we have similar philosophies. If you are a Wing T guy looking for ways to "Modernize" your offense, or a Spread guy looking for an effective and efficient run game this is the offense you should be looking at!"
Coach Sheffer

"Most offensive systems you must have really good players to run them, but with Coach Simpson's 'Gun-T' RPO system, you can be very successful just manipulating defenses with the X's & O's." –
Steven Swinson, Indiana Weslyian University

"As a traditional wing T coach for over 30 years I was looking for a package to add to my offense in order to force defense's to defend width and depth. Coach Simpson's Gun-T RPO offense does exactly that with the built in "what if then" RPO's and RRO's."
Coach Brissette

"The Gun T RPO System really helped us evolve our wing T offense and really put defenses in conflict. This system helped us break a 20 game losing streak and finish with a winning record for the first time since 2014."
Tom Mulligan, Head Coach Elmwood Park High School, Elmwood Park, New Jersey

Thank Yous

Coach Simpson and Coach Gould

It still amazes us that some high school coaches in Arkansas have been blessed to meet coaches across the country and even the world. We are so thankful to those that have supported these efforts and allowed us to travel places and meet people we'd never imagined having the opportunity to meet. Thank you so much for the support.

We also have such a good inner circle of people that don't laugh at some of the outside the box ideas we come up with, but instead support me. Our wives are the best at keeping us grounded, but supporting us in any way possible. Our children have now grown up shipping books, going to clinics with us and encouraging us as this new venture has arrived.

We are also very blessed with a great support staff at our "normal" jobs. A great administration that allows us to do things than many coaches are not afforded the opportunity to attempt. Coaches on the staff that have embraced doing things differently and taken on responsibilities to help. We've also had players that have supported these efforts.

When people do different things, there will always be thoughts of failure or embarrassment. But we've been so fortunate to have surrounded ourselves with those that encourage risk taking. And we hope if you are reading this book, you will also. Take that chance to do what you love!

Table of Contents

Introduction:	6
Overview:	9
Alignment:	13
Grading System:	19
Importance of Drills:	23
Warm up Drills:	31
Hands/Core:	33
Footwork Drills:	34
Every Day Drills:	41
Stance:	43
Down Block Drills:	47
2nd Level:	56
Pull Drills:	63
Pull-Kick:	64
Pull-Log:	68
Pull-Wrap:	70
Base Blocks:	75
Reach Block:	80
Gap-Hinge:	82
Cut Drill:	85
Steal Block Drill:	86
Chute Drills:	89
POD Drills:	95
Hurdle Drill:	97
Spacial Blocking:	102
Counter Pod:	108
Trojan Pod:	110
Double Team Drill:	113
Pass Protection:	117
Conclusion:	124
About the Authors:	125

Introduction

Coaching the offensive line is a challenge for any team. This group must be motivated to play hard, understand their rules against multiple fronts and talent levels. And they never get the recognition of a skill player. To top it all off, many times they are blamed when a play goes wrong!

But most coaches understand that to win games, you must win in the trenches. The Gun T System is set up to give linemen tools to succeed, regardless of the opposition. We want our players to have techniques they can use against any opponent.

The first portion of this book will discuss how we work with and choose our linemen. What are some quick adjustments we can make to help them do their job? Who plays where? What can we do with alignment to help?

The rest of this book will be filled with drills that we use in the Gun T Offense. Each drill has the following:

Coaching Points
Common Mistakes
Pictures and Descriptions of the drill
How the drill is used in a game

While running drills is important, understanding WHY a drill helps win games is even more important. Make sure that your players understand the purpose of each drill and how it will directly translate to the games.

Introduction

The Gun T Offense is set up much like the Wing-T in terms of blocking rules, but the technique we have had to face forces us to make some adjustments based off of the timing of the offense.

This system is set up to give smaller players an opportunity to succeed. While we want to play physical and aggressive at all times, we also understand that in many games we may be physically outmatched and these drills and tips have helped our offense run the ball against much larger and faster defenses each season.

It is our hope that as you go through these drills your offense becomes much more effective. If you have questions feel free to reach out to

Coach Gould
Email - coachbogould@gmail.com
Twitter @coachbogould
Phone # (870) 834-4889

Coach Simpson -
Email - FBCoachsimpson@gmail.com
Twitter - @FBCoachsimpson

The full system is available here:

Overview of the Oline

When running this offense we do not view all offensive lineman as the same. Each of our positions require different skill sets and we want to maximize those skills. This is also how we will set up our drill time.

While each lineman must accomplish basic skills, the time dedicated to each skill varies based off the position and the plays we wish to emphasize each season. This past season we did not even double team due to our lack of size.

Be sure to give your line tools to win. And also give them the ability to "lose" but have your team still win. For example if we are downblocking on a 330 lb player with a 185 lb player. What are the non-negotiables? Where is the play going? How can we cheat to get him sealed?

Then be sure to drill this with your player. Players will play hard for you if they know you can give them answers when things get tough. This requires film study and some flexibility in your blocking, but it will be rewarded.

It is my belief that the most selfless position in all of major sports is the offensive line. They receive the least credit when things go well and get the most blame when things go bad. Their entire goal is to help other succeed.

As you look at the drills in the book, understand that we do not give each linemen equal time on these. An undersized guard is not going to spend much time working double team drills, and a slow-footed tackle is not going to work pulling much. We would rather work out scheme to fit the skill set of each lineman and then become as good as possible on those skills.

"Everyone is a genius. But if you judge a fish by its ability to climb a tree, it will live its whole life believing that it is stupid."
Anonymous

Overview of the Oline

Below is what we look for in our linemen and tight-end. The "Y" is our tight-end and the "Q" stands for Quick, the "S" for Strong.

Y – Tight-end. Must be able to block defensive lineman. His job is crucial on buck. We generally pick our 3rd guard for this spot. If he has the ability to catch the ball that is great, but he must be a willing and able blocker for this offense to work.

QG – Most important lineman on the team. He needs to be your most athletic player on the line. Size is secondary. He will be pulling on almost all strong side runs. When you decide who goes where, start at this position. We have succeeded with a 265lb pulling guard and a 165lb guard. Blocking in space and understanding how to pull wrap are the skills needed.

SG – Second most important lineman on the team. He will pull kick most of the time, but needs to be athletic enough to wrap for Quick Belly. Usually the stronger, not as athletic of the two guards.

QT – Next most important lineman. What his skill set brings to the table will allow you (or not) to run to the quick side and all your RPO game on the backside. He also needs to be able to get in space on screen and get to second level on RPO game.

C – Must be very consistent at snapping for the offense to run smoothly. Usually this is a smart kid that can call the fronts and is able to handle backside blocking. If he is not as great a blocker, we can give help, but if he is a solid blocker it makes the scheme much easier to achieve.

ST – Usually this is a very physical, but not as athletic tackle. Often for us this is our biggest lineman. If he played at the college level he would have to play guard since often these types of bodies struggle with speed. Must be able to down block, double team and cut/hinge on backside runs.

Overview of the Oline

This is our base alignment in our offense. We flop the strong side with our "Y" if we wanted to go "strong left" or in our offense "blue".

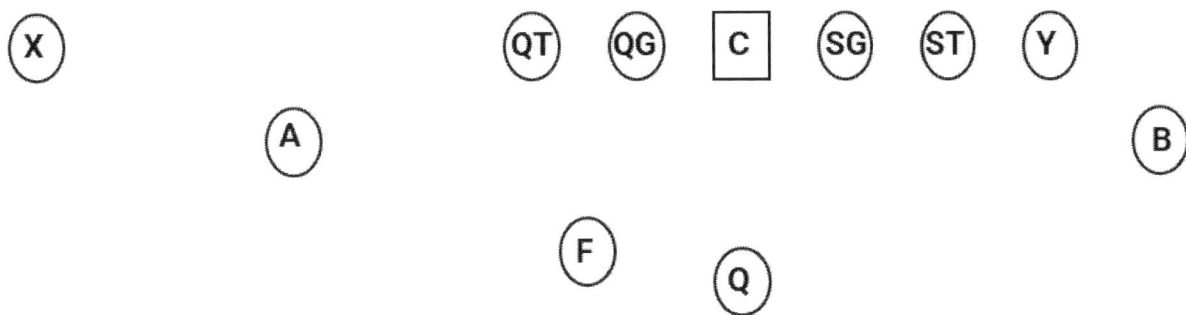

There are multiple resources as to our philosophy into using a "strong and quick" side, but generally the thought process boils down to these reasons:

1) Many kids at the high school level are limited in their abilities and by putting them on one side or another we can maximize the types of blocks they are gifted to perform.

1) This makes learning the offense much quicker as we run schemes to both sides and do not have to teach linemen each play both ways, we simply flop the line.

1) We can now play smaller/quicker players that would have difficulty blocking large linemen at the quick guard spot. We can also play slower players at 1-2 spots on the line and allow them to succeed as we only ask them to down block or hinge block.

Overview of the Oline

The premise of this offense is for a team that may be outmatched physically, to give their players tools to succeed. There will be some years that our line is big and talented, but most seasons our line has deficiencies that we must adapt our scheme to fit.

We ask our players to "block half a man" on down blocks and base blocks. We also teach angles on kick-out blocks and pull wraps. We do not want to get into a game that our line cannot do their job - regardless of the size of the opponent.

This is one of my favorite pictures with one of our 180lb guards down blocking a 340lb defensive lineman. We could never ask that player to zone block or drive block this player, but we can block "half a man" and seal him for our running back to be successful. The goal of this system is to allow a team to run the ball by understanding angles and "cheats" we give our line.

Alignment

Overview Alignment

While our offense is very much Wing-T based in it's run game, many of these concepts in this section should apply to many gap-scheme run attacks. We teach two types of alignment (or splits).

The first is "vertical" alignment. Or simply put, how close the lineman's helmet is to the line of scrimmage (or the ball before the snap). We NEVER want to cheat this alignment up. Gain as much space as possible off the line. This will clean up a multitude of issues:

1)   Helps pullers and hides who is pulling
2)   Helps slower lineman and eliminates stunts
3)   Allows cut blocks to be much more effective
4)   Creates much better angles for down blocking
5)   Helps to eliminate as much penetration as the defensive line must now take multiple steps to make contact with the offensive line.

Vertical Alignment

This is an example of "vertical" alignment. We want our lineman to put their heads on the hip of the center. This helps with our angles and with our ability to pull in space.

If it is not coached, you will have issues getting pullers out into their lanes as they will need to gain even more depth. Another issue you may face will be that the guards will want to cheat deep, but the tackles cheat up. This will be a tendency the opponent will find if not addressed.

Horizontal Alignment

This type of alignment we call our "horizontal" splits. We will adjust these season to season and even game to game or play to play.

While this may cause some tendencies, the defense does not have much time to pick up on them and the coach on the sideline cannot see this alignment well. These "cheats" have been very helpful for us as we often have very undersized linemen each week.

Feel free to adjust as needed, or do not cheat splits if you feel they are not needed by your players. We have always worked to give our players as many tools as possible to get the job done, and this has been a great addition.

General "rules" for these -
1) If we are pulling multiple players - cheat in
2) If we are running an inside run - cheat out
3) If we are double teaming - cheat together

Horizontal Alignment

Each year we must adjust to our personnel. In some years (top picture) we have a very large and talented offensive line. In other years (bottom picture) our line may be much smaller. We do not want to have an offense that only works based on the talent and size of the offensive line. We must have answers for those "down" years.

One is our "horizontal" splits. Staying off the line allows us to handle penetration and get better angles on our down blocks each season. The goal of our line is to create space horizontally.

On years our offensive line is larger (or slower) we will cheat our splits in and shrink the ability for the defense to shoot a gap.

On seasons that our line is quicker and smaller, we will cheat for wider splits.

Smart Splits Alignment

Here are some examples of "smart" splits or cheating our splits with our line to create space.

We teach this with gap concepts or RPO game with the linemen to the point that they will understand how to use splits to help them. This goes along with teaching them the base concepts and what we are trying to accomplish with creating space with gaps, not upfield push.

In the second picture we are running strong side belly.

Grading Linemen

Grading Linemen

We are very simple with grading our players. We want to keep it realistic on our sheet and provide real feedback.

Basically, we grade effort (1 point) and technique (1 point). While we do give a "grade", we also realize that some games and/or tasks are more difficult than others.

To that end we offer a quick section for notes on MAJOR areas. As coaches we can "over-coach" our players. It is best to give the most important areas we did well and areas we can improve upon. One of the biggest mistakes a coach can make is to tell their players TOO MUCH information. Focus on the biggest and most important areas they need to improve.

Also, be sure to talk about the most important areas they are doing well in.

We use this sheet and write notes on issues - once we recognize the same issue multiple times, we will give that with our grade to the lineman.

Game Type:	Date:	Opponent:	Team Blocking Totals	Team Grade
Name	Plays	Effort	Assignment	Grade
Johnny Player	48	45/48	42/48	87/96 = 91%

Grading Linemen

Below you will see an example of what we give our players in our weekly scouting report. Earlier in the year we may give them a couple more coaching notes, this is an example of late in the year.

Again, keeping with the theme of simple you do not want to give them too much. Pick one or two things to work on and one or two things they did well.

Stevens - More consistent working your feet after contact. (Understanding where to lose and staying connected)

Hedden - More consistent with your first step. (Fast and gain grown, rather than slow and pivot)

Foster - More consistent blocking rules with various fronts. (Blocking back when needed)

Hodge - More consistent on reads. (Stay on first contact)

Tate - More consistent on kick outs. (Pull right hit right, pull left hit left)

Manning/Cartwright/Henrickson - Another strong practice week for you, continue to be ready.

Y -
Good job last week, you are becoming a weapon that teams are working to cover. Keep blocking well and we will find ways to involve you in the passing game.

Drills

Drills

When we begin to build our drills for the offensive line, we start with a priority list. It is easy to spend massive amounts of time on drills that may not really translate to what they need to accomplish. To this end we have some drills that every lineman must go through and we will work these everyday. You will find many of these drills in this section.

However, we also have a few drills that are specifically for our guards and tight ends since they are the only ones we ask to pull in our offense. Those drills we attempt to always accomplish in our "POD" time. When we build a practice, we start with drills each lineman needs to do.

We then work on drills that are the most important for us that season. Since we know Buck and Counter will be in our playbook each season, we work **down blocks** very often. If we are going to run a lot of Belly, we will be sure to work our **base blocks** and **double team blocks**. If we feel we will be a heavy screen team, we will work **spatial blocking** and so-on.

Basically, be sure to prioritize these drills to match the plays you feel will be you most important plays in a given season and adjust as you go. Many of these drills are common place, but what we hope makes our practice time and drills unique, is that we work hard to explain the "why" to our players. When they understand *why a drill will help them be successful*, they are much more likely to work hard at that drill.

This offense is designed to move people sideways and create space and gaps. While we will adjust each season, our goal is to create space each season regardless of the matchups we may face. Many of these drills can be adapted to your system or players, but this manual will walk through most of the "base" ways we teach them.

"There are no shortcuts to building a team each season. You build the foundation brick by brick."
Bill Belichick

Drills

Another way we build our drill book is through plays. For example, these are the drills that help often with Buck and Counter. We must be able to Down Block and Pull.

When we go to our "POD" time we will split the linemen into groups so that they can work on each portion of this blocking scheme. The guards on pulling and the rest of the line on down blocking.

Often, these drills are being run at the same time - the guards are pulling and the rest are working on our downblock drills.

As you go through the manual, you will see that these drills will be listed individually, but often we will have 2-3 drills happening simultaneously.

Drill Time

When we evaluate what drills to run with our linemen, they are not all equal! We want to see which types of blocks the player will be required to make. If they play guard in our offense, they will usually work much more on pulling than our tackles. While our tackles will need more time on Down/Hinge and other types of blocks.

On the next page is an in-season practice schedule and you will see that our linemen are all working throughout the practice, but each position is working on the drills that will help them succeed.

Each linemen has certain skills needed - Stance, Down Blocks, Etc…

But not each linemen needs to perform each block, and some need to perform specific blocks more than others.

Be sure to allocate the time for them to work the skill needed in your practice plans.

Another "cheat" we use for our linemen, is to "steal" time during special teams work. While we may not have all our linemen (as some could be long snappers, etc…), we should have the majority of them available. This allows this position group to get an additional 5-15 minutes per day to work on individual drills.

Drill time should be sacred time for the offensive line and their coach. This time is key in developing the skills needed. There is always something to improve upon and we should never "rush" through the drills. As the season progresses and we shrink our practice time, the offensive line must begin to allocate additional time to improve and make very wise use of their time. On the following pages are a few of our in-season schedules.

Practice Schedule

PD	QB	F	Y/B	X and A	OL	DL	ILB
1	Specialty and Indy work - Punters/Kickers/Holders/Snappers/Returners/Kick Blockers						Non specialt
2	BREAK						
3	Special Team Install #1		PUNT	Gunners with Denton - Weaver/Simpson on protection and lane			
4							
5	Special Team Install #2		XP	Gate Install with Gould			
6							
7	BREAK						
8	FTWK	Ball Drills	DOWN	Ball Drills	Down Blocks	Defense only with Denton/Ay	
9	Fire Route	Blocking (R/L)	Ball Drill	Fire Route	Rock/Load	Film Room reviewing blit	
10	Cannon / Trojan POD		Cannon	Review Smash	TE/B/ST/C buck adjusts QT with Fox Steal call		
11	Work QB/Train/Rotate QB's		Trojan	Work Connie	Cuts		

This is an example of a practice schedule from this season. On the offensive line section start with period 8.

Period 8: ALL linemen are working down blocks (skill)

Period 9: ALL linemen are working our Rock/Load protections (scheme)

Period 10: We begin our "POD" time: Guards go with the backs to work our run concepts. The Strong Tackle, Center, Tight End and Wing are working down blocks specific to "Buck". The Quick Tackle is working the "Steal" footwork.

Period 11: Still in POD with the guards. But now our ST/C/QT are working cut blocks. Our TE/Wing are working Trojan blocks.

While we have many flavors each day, this is a similar set up:
1) Work a skill (EDD)
2) Work a scheme (in season)
3) Work our POD's (specific work for each position)

Practice Schedule

PD	QB	F	Y/B	X and A	OL
1	Specialty		QB - Gameplan, Line working stance		
2	BREAK				
3	Roll and read OLB	Ball Drill	Trojan	Ball Drill	Down Blocks
4	POD Period - F's (B's), QG and Q's		Y - Down Blocks	Screens - B's	DBL Teams
5	Roll out game	Rodeo/Lasso	PA Pass	Roll out game	Rodeo/Lasso
6	PACE PERIOD - Simpson (mix in Nascars)				
7	BREAK				

Here is another example of a practice schedule in-season. Time is limited as our players go both ways.

We are "stealing" time during period 1 to work on stance (could also do ladder drills). This is a great time to also do overview of the defense if limited even more in time.

Period 3 - we are working down blocks with all our linemen - we can mix in 2nd level on this period as well.

Period 4 - we are working our pull wraps with our Quick Guards - we could take both guards here as well - and our other linemen are working double teams. Often, if possible we would send our Quick Tackle to work his RPO blocks.

Period 5 - we are working with our line and "F" on Rodeo/Lasso protection.

The rest of the practice is team time and situational football as we were in-season. Early in the season or during the preseason we would go longer in individual time.

Drills

These are our top drills we will run with our line each year. In each drill you will find:

1) Purpose and Skill we are working on
2) Set up of the drill
3) Coaching points to give
4) Common mistakes to avoid

I have also labeled which linemen (from all to "guards") need to be working a drill. We want to make sure that we are working the drills that matter and spending the most time on the most important drills.

Each season, coaches will adapt their play-calling, but I have ordered the most common way we would prioritize our drills in this section.

It is VITAL, that a coach ensures his players understand the "why" of the drill. They must understand how this drill translates directly to their success on the field.

Warm up Drills

Warm up Drills

These first few drills are what we like to do during our pre-practice or during specialty time. They are a great way to work skills all linemen need, but are not scheme related, as we are often missing players that may be working a specialty skill.

As a team we usually do not start practice by standard stretches, but instead often will use these types of drills as our "warm-up" period.

These drills are also usually the first few we will run during the off-season to work on evaluating our linemen.

These can be run without pads.

As the season progresses, we do not run these drills or run them as often, unless they were to be needed or used as a warm-up drill.

HANDS/CORE DRILL
ALL LINEMEN

PURPOSE
To teach keeping our hands inside and maintaining balance.

Good warm up drill

I want to acknowledge this is from "Tip of the Spear" as a good drill for leverage.

KEY SKILLS
Balanced Stance
Hands inside
Core and arm strength

SETUP
Done in partners

DRILL INSTRUCTIONS
Players will partner-up and put hands as if the are praying.

The partner will push and try to knock them off-balance

COMMON MISTAKES
Players lean to contact instead of keep balance

Base is too narrow

COACHING POINTS
Good warm up drill or drill to teach hands inside and balance.

Ladder Drills

Ladder Drills
- One foot every hole
- Two feet every hole
- Shuffle Forward
- Shuffle Backward
- Linebacker Shuffle
- Skiers
- Scissors

These ladder drills will help each player develop coordination, have faster feet, and get use to taking shorter steps.

Start as slow as you want while teaching the steps, pick up speeds as they get used to it (mainly on the shuffle steps).

As you build up the goal is to be able to them without looking down.

Hands tight and elbows squeezed, as well as staying low are also key coaching points.

These drills are good for any linemen an any offense. In our system they serve as a good warmup that we like to use during specialty to get our guys moving and active.

We do not always do each of the ladder drills, depending on the time we have. The goal is simple - working to get our players warmed up for practice, while also working on balance and quickness.

These drills can also be done without a ladder, simply using the hash marks on the field.

The other drills are very similar, with a different movement.

To view these drills video follow this QR Code:

One Foot Every Hole

ALL LINEMEN

PURPOSE
To develop the proper footwork that is essential to lineman.

KEY SKILLS
Balance
Quick Feet
Low base

SETUP
Ladder on level ground. Coach where he can see players perform proper techniques.

DRILL INSTRUCTIONS
- Start outside the ladder.
- Stepping one foot in each hole.
- Feet should land fast and loud, with all cleats in the ground.
- Hands tight elbows squeezed.
- Bend in knees. Maintaining leverage.

COMMON MISTAKES
- Players are on toes. Rather than heavy with feet.
- Do not have proper hand placement.
- Staying too high.

COACHING POINTS
- Always have hands tight and elbows squeezed.
- Loud, Heavy feet.
- At first players can have eyes down, as they get comfortable eyes are up.

Two Feet Every Hole

ALL LINEMEN

PURPOSE
To develop the proper footwork that is essential to lineman.

KEY SKILLS
Balance
Quick Feet
Low base

SETUP
Ladder on level ground. Coach where he can see players perform proper techniques.

DRILL INSTRUCTIONS
- Start outside the ladder
- Step one will be into the ladder section.
- Step two will be into them same ladder section as the first.
- Continue to move forward, while landing both feet in each ladder section one after the other.

COMMON MISTAKES
- Players are on toes, without all cleats in the ground.
- Feet are too close together.
- Do not have proper hand placement.
- Players are too high.

COACHING POINTS
- Always have hands tight and elbows squeezed.
- Loud, Heavy feet.
- At first players can have eyes down, as they get comfortable eyes are up.

Step One

Step Two

Shuffle Forward
ALL LINEMEN

PURPOSE
To develop the proper footwork that is essential to lineman.

KEY SKILLS
Balance
Quick Feet
Low base

SETUP
Ladder on level ground. Coach where he can see players perform proper techniques.

DRILL INSTRUCTIONS
- Start outside of the ladder to the side, while facing forward.
- From there you will shuffle sideways using the In, In, Out method inside each ladder box.
- Continue with this method until reaching the end of the ladders.

COMMON MISTAKES
- Feet will cross, rather than remain apart.
- Will be on toes.
- Get confused what foot comes next.

COACHING POINTS
- Same coaching points as other ladder drills.
- This one will take longer for the player to master. Be patient as they work through it.

Ladder

Shuffle Backwards

Same instructions as shuffle forwards. The only thing that will change is the players will shuffle backwards, rather than forward.

Good drill for pass protection.

Also, have patience this will be the longest one to master.

Picture below will give you the idea of how it is laid out.

Ladder

Skiers and Scissors

These two ladder drills are designed to increase speed and agility.

The previous ladder drills had the coaching point of hands tight and elbows squeezed. These will vary. Scissors will be pumping your arms (like you are running), while Skiers hand placement will vary to keep balance. **See the pictures below.**

Coaching Points (Scissors)
- Alternate feet while pumping arms and moving down the ladder.
- DO NOT drag feet!

Coaching Points (Skiers)
- Feet are together.
- Moving in the box and then out of the box.
- Some call these bunny hops.

Ladder

Steps on Skiers

- Start with both feet outside.
- Feet stay together while doing the jumps and moving in and out of the ladders.
- Continue these movements thru the end of the ladder

Steps on Scissors

- Start in staggered stance.
- Switching feet and pumping arms down the ladder. Face the same way on the way back.
- Players should jump off ground and not slide or scoot feet.

Every-Day Drills

E.D.D.

These are our "EDD" or Every-Day Drills. We want to get these in every day in the spring/summer and at least on 2-3 days each week. Often, we will build these drills into our "warm-up" period.

These are drills that every lineman and our "Y" need to get often. They are not position specific, but drills for every spot on the line. We will work these the first day we begin working "football" and continue though the last week we play.

The biggest challenge in these drills is to not become "bored" but to focus on why they are important. Work hard to make sure your athletes understand why they need these drills. As the season goes on, these drills are still worked on, but we may shrink our time as our players have grown comfortable with them.

Be sure to invest the time on the front end to explain how this drill helps your team win and this will help create buy-in from your players. The best way to get players to believe is to be able to explain simply to them how what you are teaching can give them success.

Our main drills we work each day:

Stance
Steps
Down Blocks
Pulls

Stance

We are a Wing T based blocking team, so our stance will reflect that. If your offense is not, simply adjust this to reflect what you would like. However, each line coach should be working stance/starts every day in any style of offense.

We will spend 5-10 minutes each day in the spring and early season on stance. As the season progresses, we will still work stance, but usually pair it with a drill working 1st or 1st and 2nd steps.

Stance should always be worked on, but as the season progresses, it is usually coached with another drill/concept.

STANCE DRILL
ALL LINEMEN

PURPOSE
To teach our line balance in their stances. We will adjust based on personnel, but want to teach a few key components.

KEY SKILLS
Balanced stance
Ability to block down or pull
Weight distribution

SETUP
Can be done with a chute
Can be done with hurdles
Can be done with partners

DRILL INSTRUCTIONS
Coaches will stand behind the players and use partners (if no chute is available) to work on keeping their shoulders down. We want to work on a forward bend with little weight on our hands. Would like feet shoulder width to slightly wider. We teach our inside hands down.

COMMON MISTAKES
Feet too wide
Weight too far forward
Bending at waist, but not at knees

COACHING POINTS
Start with leaning forward in a 2 point stance and then let the hand drag the ground. In the bottom picture we probably have too much weight forward.

44

Stance and Steps
All Lineman

PURPOSE
To teach lineman proper balance, while having fast first steps. Also they will learn how to step at angles.

KEY SKILLS
Balanced Stance
Stepping at angles
Fast First Step
Staying low
Steps include (On Step, Gap Step, Down Step, and Pull Step.

SETUP
Can be done with a chute
Can be done with hurdles
Can be done with partners

DRILL INSTRUCTION
Players and coaches will align as shown to the right. Each of the following steps are one step and then reset in proper stance. Coach will yell the step and players will wait for cadence to the step.

COMMON MISTAKES
Players will pop up rather than stay low.

Slow off the ball

Players will pivot step rather than gaining ground.

COACHING POINTS
Go slow at first. Give time to get set up in stance. As you go get faster with your commands. Make sure they gain ground and stay low on steps.

PLUS DRILL
ALL LINEMEN

PURPOSE
First step
We are working on staying low coming out of our stance
6 inch step

KEY SKILLS
Weight stays centered
Short step
STAY LOW

SETUP
Preferably on an "X" on the field

Need a line

Chute or Partners

DRILL INSTRUCTIONS
We will set up on an "X" if possible to highlight the step. If we are working with a large group we want them on a line.

If done with partners we want to make the goal to stay low.

6 inch step on a down block is main goal..

COMMON MISTAKES
Too big a step
Raise up
Lean forward too much .

COACHING POINTS
Work on keeping the "bend in the knees"

Stay low by bending, not lunging

Short step to keep balance

Down Blocks

Down Block

The down block is one of the most important blocks within a spread power offense. Lineman, TE, and Wings will all perform this block. To achieve this block players will have to understand the following concepts

1. **Where the play is going.** By understanding this the player will know where the defender can not go. We also refer to this as knowing how to lose.

1. **Blocking Rule.** Most common rule that involves a down block is gap, down, backer. Therefore the player will have a different approach if blocking a lineman vs a linebacker.

1. **What kind of player is the defender.** This will change aiming points, footwork, and technique.

We work down blocks - some variation - every day. This is vital to our offense as every player must be great at blocking down for our offense to work. This next section will go through many flavors of drills to accomplish the same idea - blocking down. If the offense is not good at this skill, nothing else matters. Spend the time to be great on blocking down, before moving into other types of blocks.

For video on some of the drills:

Down Block

Down Block for "Heel Line" Defenders

We struggled very much with "over the top" players on Buck/Outside runs

This drill will force OL/TE/Wing to work hips to sideline

We call it "over the top" --- Goal is for all down blockers to end up with their butt to the end zone we are working towards

The "defenders" are also holding their arm out to help our linemen stay low throughout the drill. We want to stay on the opponents hip to get movement.

We have taught putting our head on the backside of the defender, if they are not attempting to get penetration, but simply staying on the line of scrimmage. We want to "wash them down" or seal them inside.

Down Block

Down Block for "Up-field" Defenders

When playing a team that relies on penetration, we will work flatter steps in this drill and stress getting our head across the defender.

We will often have the "defenders" (players) step forward at the snap to change the angle for our down block. This is done to help our players understand how they must step flatter to make the block.

The goal here is to get our "head across" which should cause us to step flatter and handle the penetration.

DOWN BLOCK (Overview)
ALL LINEMEN

PURPOSE
Teaching how to block down on a first level defender

KEY SKILLS
Maintaining balance

Working the defender down and keeping body between them and ball carrier

SETUP
Done with partners that will off-set to be "down" for our linemen.

Use hands to encourage low pad level

DRILL INSTRUCTIONS
We like to do this with partner set up and in increments of steps.

Plus drill and then we add step 2 and then future steps

We want to step and get head to the hip of the defender and use outside hand to keep them inside.

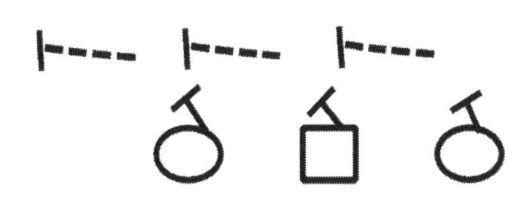

COMMON MISTAKES
Stepping upfield too far

Too large steps

Not bringing outside hand to drive defenders.

COACHING POINTS
We teach 2 types of defenders (previous pages) and that will adjust aiming point, but early on we focus on upfield teams.

6 inch steps and turn body in a 180 by end of the drill..

DOWN BLOCK 1st Step
ALL LINEMEN

PURPOSE
Teaching the first step of a down block.

KEY SKILLS
Maintaining balance
Taking short steps
Aiming point for body

SETUP
Done with partners that will off-set to be "down" for our linemen.

Use hands to encourage low pad level

DRILL INSTRUCTIONS
We like to do this with partner set up. Can also be done under a hurdle.

Gain ground with the first step. Heel replaces toe at an angle.

Pad level stays the same.

Lineman will load/hulster hands.

COMMON MISTAKES
Too big of a first step, thus throwing off balance.

Player will raise out of stance or pop up.

Hands too wide and not on holster area.

COACHING POINTS
Having the short initial step is crucial for a successful down block as well as low pad level. Training this way helps with both of those..

DOWN BLOCK First two steps
ALL LINEMEN

PURPOSE
Teaching the first two steps of a down block.

KEY SKILLS
Maintaining balance
Taking short steps
Aiming point for body

SETUP
Done with partners that will off-set to be "down" for our linemen.

Use hands to encourage low pad level

DRILL INSTRUCTIONS
We like to do this with partner set up. Can also be done under a hurdle or s chute.

Follow the guidelines for taking the first step.

On the second step foot should come and align with first step.

Shoulder and head should be on player and hands should fire.

COMMON MISTAKES
Too big of a first step, thus throwing off balance.

Player will raise out of stance or pop up. Need to be at same height.

Taking to big of a step throwing of balance.

COACHING POINTS
Make sure drill is done on our cadence. You can make it as fast or as slow as you want to. Pad level should not change on the first two steps. That's the reason for players arm being out.

DOWN BLOCK Run'em and Turn'em
ALL LINEMEN

PURPOSE
Putting together the complete down block and what to do after contact is made.

KEY SKILLS
Maintaining balance throughout while running feet.

SETUP
Done with partners that will off-set to be "down" for our linemen.

Add hand shields to give resistance and more contact.

DRILL INSTRUCTIONS
We like to do this with partner set up.

Follow the guidelines for taking the first two steps.

Going on a snap count now. Putting the complete down block together.

Will get push of 2-3 yards prior to turning back and working feet towards end zone.

COMMON MISTAKES
Taking negative steps.

Having sprinters feet and not appropriate base/balance.

Working feet and back to earlier. We call this spinning like a top.

COACHING POINTS
Making sure they are getting the 2-3 yards of push prior to working feet is key. This drill helps to prevent defenders from falling off blocks to make tackles.

DOWN BLOCK drill with No Hands
ALL LINEMEN

PURPOSE
Putting together the complete down block while using no hands to focus on balance and shoulder placement.

KEY SKILLS
Maintaining balance throughout while not using hands.

SETUP
Done with partners that will off-set to be "down" for our linemen.

DRILL INSTRUCTIONS
Same drill as Run'em and Turn'em, but you are not using hands.

Hands will be behind back.

Drill done on snap count.

Using no hands allows for shoulder and head to be correctly into the defender.

Stress the importance of a good base and head/shoulder placement.

COMMON MISTAKES
It will be obvious if you have a bad base now.

Players will struggle with losing balance.

Focus on first two steps as well.

COACHING POINTS
This drill helps teach the importance of head and shoulders being on the defenders. Use this to correct hands being over extended as well as correcting a bad base.

2nd LEVEL DOWN BLOCK
ALL LINEMEN

PURPOSE
Teaching Down Blocks on LB/DB players at the 2nd level of the defense. This has been very difficult for our linemen as they want to "chase" defensive players..

DRILL INSTRUCTIONS
We set up a partner line 5 yards deep. The coach will tell them on the "snap" if they remain in place or run to the outside (the reactions we see in a game).

Linemen will block the man down or if he leaves they stay on the path an block the next partner..

COMMON MISTAKES
Linemen chase their partner

The angle they take is too flat

Don't settle their feet to block.

COACHING POINTS
This is a spacial type of block so we must gather our balance and use our hands and leverage.

Don't chase the LB if he flys over the top.

KEY SKILLS
Learning to block an area and not chase a man.

Coming to "balance" to block a skilled defender.

SETUP
Partners back up 5 yards and 2-3 yards inside.

Coach gives direction to "stay" or work over the top to the "defense".

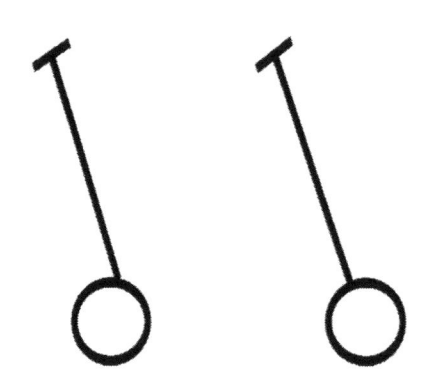

2nd Level Down Block

Drill set up can be multiple. This is an example of one coach with a large group of players. The "live" players are on the side with the coach, while the other side is simulating the reaction the the defense. The aiming point is the upfield hip, or a man over. We want to ensure we take a down step first, this helps to ensure we stay on our tracks if a blitzer or stunter shows late.

The picture below is an example of the coach telling the defense to "stay" or not move. The other options would be to attack the gap or to play a scrape technique - over the top. We teach our linemen to take a good angle, but if the defender runs away, do not veer off your path.

2nd Level Down Block

This is the hip we would like to attack. We want to turn our back to the sideline and seal the defender inside on all 2nd level down blocks. The goal is to adjust to the defender and get the "seal" inside. The picture on the bottom right shows a great example of this block in action.

2nd Level Down Block

This is an example of the defenders playing "scrape" technique. We will take the angle towards their upfield hip, but DO NOT CHASE. Instead we should work to the backside player.

This is a picture showing the players working to the backside player.

2nd Level Down Block

Down blocking on the second level is much more about understanding leverage of the defense. This is an example of our wing blocking down on an inside linebacker. Notice he steps flat to the block, if the LB shoots he is ready.

Once he identifies the LB is playing over the top he re-positions to his back hip to seal him inside. This run resulted in a touchdown, due to this block and seal.

2nd Level Down Block

This is a good example of a young lineman working for a 2nd level down block. He is at the far right of the first picture as his aiming point took him to a playside LB that read very quickly and moved past him.

Instead of chasing him, he worked to the backside LB - #48. Notice he is working to where the LB will go as he shuffles his feet and maintains his balance. The second picture shows him picking up the LB and sealing him off.

Pull Drills

For video on some of the drills:

PULL KICK

POSITION: Guards and Tightends

PURPOSE

Teaching our linemen to kick a force player

Used with buck/counter

DRILL INSTRUCTIONS

We will usually work this with hurdles to create an obvious target

We want our linemen to "pull the lawn mower" and get 3 depth steps and then move TOWARDS THE LINE as they kick the force player.

COMMON MISTAKES

Linemen are not tight enough to the line and allow force player inside.

Don't get depth on first 3 steps

Slow down on contact.

COACHING POINTS

Hit with same shoulder in direction you ar pulling – Pull Right, Hit Right

Run through the block

Come "downhill" to create a great angle.

Do not slow down – force defender to run upfield.

KEY SKILLS

Teaching leverage on kicks

Speed and footwork

Angles of the pull

SETUP

We prefer oversized hurdles, but can use bags or cones.

Want to do this on a line.

At times we will cone off the area to force depth on first 3 steps.

Pull Kick

OL → BAG/DL

Pull Kick

To help teach this skill, we have added in a coach/partner "hand slap". This helps us to teach aiming points on a moving target. It also encourages our players to move "through the block" on kicks. If you look to the right of this picture, you can see the players is slapping the correct hand of the coach.

In the picture below, you can see how the drill translates to the game, as our guard is kicking out a defender with his head on the correct shoulder. We also use the phrase - "Pull Right, Kick Right" or "Pull Left, Kick Left". The idea is to get our head on the correct shoulder to ensure the player is kicked out and we can run underneath.

Pull Kick

The kick-out block is key in buck sweep in our offense and in counter and power in most other offenses. This is a clear example of coming down-hill and attacking the correct shoulder. Look at the gap that is created as we "pull left, hit left" on this kick. The gap will be widened as we run through the defender.

We want to strike quickly and with the correct leverage. We are fine if we "miss" as long as the defender works up-field. The next page will show what to do after contact.

Here is the next clip of the same block. The defender is sealed out and he cannot escape inside. The goal of our kick out is to create a seal and not allow him back over our inside shoulder. Once contact is made, we want to push him up-field as shown in this picture. Notice the guard has his hand on the back hip of the force player and is escorting him up-field and out of the play.

The defender can run as far up-field as possible, we simply do not want him to cross our face and get into the hole we have now created.

Pull Kick

While we want to have clean blocks and wide gaps to run through in our offense, that is not often realistic depending on our athletes or the opposition. In this example we a "miss" from our guard on the kick out block.

We tell our players if we are going to miss, we want to miss on the upfield shoulder of the defender, because like this picture illustrates, the defender has taken himself out of the play and ability to make a tackle by going upfield.

While we don't want to miss a block, we want to over-emphasize getting to the upfield shoulder on all kick out blocks. If we "miss" that way, our play still works. But if we "miss" on the wrong shoulder, it will cause no running room for our wrapping guard and running back.

PULL LOG

POSITION: Guards and Tightends

PURPOSE

Teaching our linemen to Log a force player

Used with buck/counter

DRILL INSTRUCTIONS

Learning when to log (seal) a player

Coach/Scout player will step very flat down the line – DO NOT GET UPFIELD

Pulling linemen will run to same spot as kick, but when he doesn't have the angle will work to seal – run his feet and force inside.

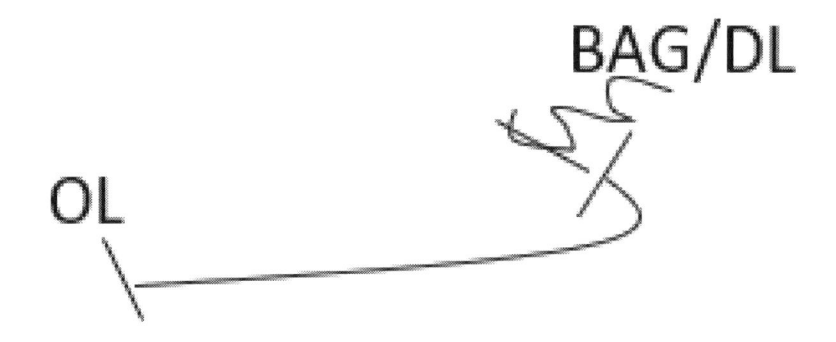

Common Mistakes

Linemen will anticipate the log and run deeper than normal.

Feet will stop on contact and no seal is ever made

KEY SKILLS

Teaching leverage

Understand how to read defensive player

How to "seal" a crashing defensive player

SETUP

We want to run this with a coach if possible so they can see how and when to log a player.

Coach will step flat and not allow space for a kick.

COACHING POINTS

We want to kick everything, so run to kick and react to log.

Once the kick has failed, run feet in a circle to seal the defender inside.

Pull Log

We do not often log, but here is an example of the same guard that was kicking a defender working his feet to seal the player.

When we identify the need to log, we want to work our feet in almost a circle and seal the defensive player inside. This is using their technique against them and is often more of a technical block.

We want to make sure this block is only used when a kick is not going to happen. Often pullers will try to do this too often since it seems easier, but it will string the play out.

PULL WRAP

POSITION: Guards and Tightends

PURPOSE
Teaching our pullers to stay on their track and not chase defensive players.

KEY SKILLS
Getting depth on pull

Getting squared to the line

Eyes inside

Staying on path

SETUP
Working with 2 "LB's" set up

Coach will signal where the linebackers will fit

Wrapping player will pick up whichever LB steps to his gap

DRILL INSTRUCTIONS
We want to use this as a way to enforce staying on our path

We will use cones to enforce depth and bags/hurdles to work on setting path, but we want bodies to create a read for our OL as they wrap.

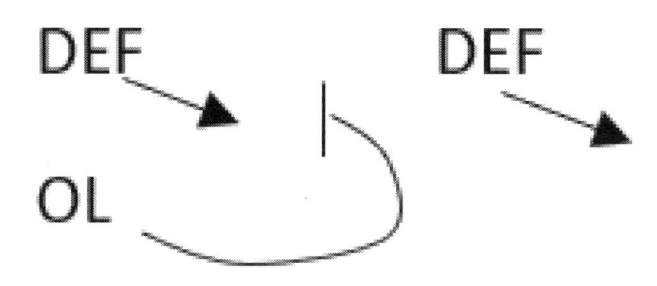

COMMON MISTAKES
Not enough depth on pull

Do not get square to line

Chasing LB instead of running path

COACHING POINTS
Get depth to get out of trash.

Take first daylight and keep eyes inside

Run your path – don't chase

Run through contact – do not slow down

Pull Wrap

DEF → | DEF →

OL ⤵

Coach

Pull Wrap

Our #1 goal in all pull-wrap blocks is to get our players eyes inside. The most common mistake we have is our eyes going wide, which causes us to not get turned up in the hole for blocks. The worst-case scenario is what we are preparing for, and that is a linebacker shooting the gap immediately. In our drill work, we work with players to aim for "half a man" with a coach. This is shown in the first picture. We will look for the hand to slap.

Here is a picture of our "trojan" play with both guards wrapping in the hole. They are working to get their eyes inside, which will get their bodies turned square and allow them to take on any filling linebacker/safety that may show up in the hole.

We want to be as tight as possible to any down blocks.

Pull Wrap

Great example of a pull wrap, as we can see the guard had created depth on his pull. He is not square to the line of scrimmage with his eyes searching inside for the linebacker/safety that will fit.

Notice he is leaning forward and is running at close to full speed as we want this to hit as quickly as possible. Remember, the running back will make him right if a defender wants to dance.

The major coaching point is to get players eyes "inside". Most of our mistakes come from not finding defenders that are tracking our ball carriers from the inside.

Pull Wrap

This is another example of getting our "eyes inside" on pull-wraps. We want to be sure to get our body turned to take on the scraping linebacker or fitting safeties. #56 is doing a great job getting his eyes towards the defender.

While there are many other aspects of wrap blocking, getting our eyes inside is the main part we work to teach.

The second part of the block for us is to attack the inside shoulder of the defender. This allow us to be prepared if he chutes to go underneath the block. It is much easier to adjust if we are tight on our pulls and aiming for the inside shoulder.

Base, Reach and Cut

Fit and Leverage
All Lineman

PURPOSE
Teaching proper fit and leverage, that essential for the success of lineman.

KEY SKILLS
Teaching to not lunge
Keeping a good, wide base
Proper finish of a block

SETUP
Can be done in pads or without. Also can add a board or dummy for proper foot placement.

DRILL INSTRUCTIONS
Start out like the picture to the right. Hands tight and elbows squeezed (FIT), top of the head under defender's chin (LEVERAGE). On cadence for forward with short choppy steps. On whistle players will extend arms and roll hips.

COMMON MISTAKES
Players will not roll hips.
Negative steps are taken at start.
Long steps and up on toes.

COACHING POINTS
Eyes on first step, making sure its not back. Make sure all cleats are in ground.

Fit and Leverage

We like to work this drill early in the season with our linemen to work on hip explosion.

While we are usually a down block and kick type of offense, there will be times we run our belly play that require linemen to "base" block.

This drill is preparing them for base blocking.

As we progress, we will work this drill from a "half-a-man" or by splitting the man in half with our feet and hands.

For the video of the drill follow the QR:

BASE BLOCK
POSITION

PURPOSE

Working on pad level and hand placement as we drive a defender.

We will work straight ahead early, but really focus on moving them horizontally.

KEY SKILLS

Keep feet moving

Fit hands inside of pads

If we are working angle, force defender and seal them and then drive

SETUP

Done with partners

Can use bags early

Can use rubber "boards" to keep feet separated.

DRILL INSTRUCTIONS

We are working our "base" block. Taking a defensive player either back or blocking them out in our offense.

Limenen come out of stance and drive feet – wide base and tight hands through the whistle.

COMMON MISTAKES

Stopping feet or taking long steps

Feet get too narrow

Grabbing outside of defenders

Raising up too quickly

COACHING POINTS

Short choppy steps

Shoulder width base

Keep hands inside

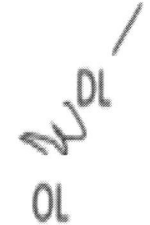

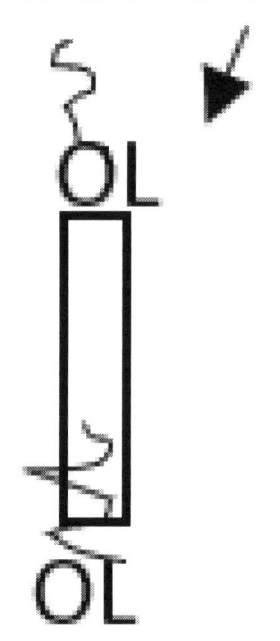

Base Block

We are not perfect on this base block, but are doing a lot of things correctly. The tackle has positioned his body to protect the hole and drive the defender out but stepping with his inside foot. He has also done a great job of keeping his hands inside of the defensive player. Finally, he is winning the leverage battle by keeping his pads lower and has good bend in his knees to drive.

One of our goals for linemen - especially undersized linemen - is to block "half a man". Or to take one shoulder and create horizontal space. We aren't as concerned with moving them upfield as we are moving them sideways.

REACH BLOCK
All Linemen

PURPOSE

Teaching Reach Blocks

We use these on Jet and a similar block on Roll-out passing..

DRILL INSTRUCTIONS

We set up in partners and ask our "Defensive Linemen" to fight upfield or outside.

When we begin this process we start in a 2-PT stance.

We will progress it to our stance and work on getting our inside hand through the outside shoulder of the DL..

COMMON MISTAKES

Feet Stop

Grabbing cloth on shoulder of DL – That will be called holding

.

COACHING POINTS

We want to work to get our inside hand through the outside of the defensive player.

Run your feet.

Do not grab.

KEY SKILLS

Teaching to Reach outside shoulder of the DL.

SETUP

This is easiest to do with partners.

Can make this easier by starting in a 2-PT stance and cheating leverage.

Progress up to stance and wide techniques. .

We will combine this with all our offensive line to work on coming off to 2nd level and staying on our track.

If we "cannot" reach the DL then we will base him out and drive him upfield as far as possible for our running back to cut back.

Reach Block

Our goal on a reach block is to get our inside hand through the defenders outside shoulder before starting to turn. This is a great example by our tackle of using his feet to get into a great position. The next part of the block would be to engage with both hands and seal the defender and drive him back.

Once we have secured the edge, we will quickly flip our hips to seal the defender inside.

In our system, we do not run much of this type of block, so often we only drill our Quick Tackle and TE/Wings on this type of block.

GAP-HINGE BLOCK
All Linemen

PURPOSE
Teaching the proper Gap-Hinge block and understanding how to protect the gap first.

KEY SKILLS
Teaching to block an area, not a man
Stepping hard inside
Forcing the defender outside

SETUP
One offensive player and two defensive players, one will be the end and the other will be a linebacker.

DRILL INSTRUCTIONS
Coach will stand behind the offensive player. He will signal to the linebacker when to blitz.

Offensive player will take inside step if no blitz will the hinge back on the lineman.

COMMON MISTAKES
Do not protect the gap first and assume they hinge.

Letting the defender cross their face, rather than running them upfield.

COACHING POINTS
Make sure the lineman does not cross the tackle's face. Run the defender upfield.

Gap-Hinge

Our goal on a reach block is to get our inside hand through the defenders outside shoulder before starting to turn. This is a great example by our tackle of using his feet to get into a great position. The next part of the block would be to engage with both hands and seal the defender and drive him back.

Gap-Hinge

This is an example of how a gap-hinge block would take on a blitzer. The quick tackle - on the left - steps into "B gap" and picks up the blitzing linebacker.

The idea is to close down the gap and if a defender appears - blitzing linebacker or stunting defensive lineman, we would pick them up. If neither appears, they would "hinge" back on the defensive end.

CUT DRILL
ALL LINEMEN

PURPOSE

Working the cut block on inside defenders.

We want to stress not simply diving.

KEY SKILLS

Going low and rolling through contact.

Keep head out of contact and learn to aim where the defensive linemen is moving toward.

SETUP

Best to use with larger dummies

Partners will off-set inside

Coach stands behind OL to watch/critique

DRILL INSTRUCTIONS

We will work partners holding bags. OL will shoot through the bag and bear-crawl and/or roll through contact.

Partners then switch.

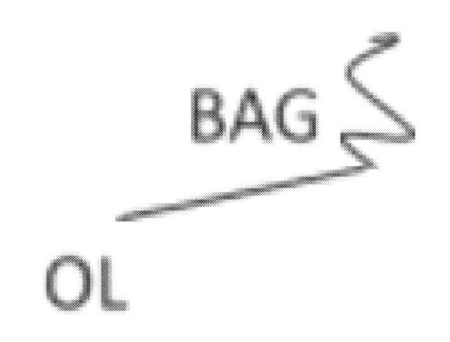

COMMON MISTAKES

Diving in wrong angle

Simply "belly flopping"

Leading with head

COACHING POINTS

Aim flatter than you want

Roll through contact

Narrow stance

STEAL BLOCK
Quick Tackles

PURPOSE
Teaching to read and react to the defenders move.

KEY SKILLS
Basic understanding of line play.

Getting eyes outside/in

SETUP
Quick Tackles and Coach are needed. Coach may need a hand shield.

DRILL INSTRUCTIONS
Coach "plays" the Outside Linebacker. Coach will do to moves. Come towards the Lineman (to force), or drop back (in coverage).

Quick Tackle
If coach steps up to play force, you would then block him.
If coach drops back to cover, you would wrap up field with eyes inside.

COMMON MISTAKES
Quick Tackle will try to get a "kill" shot on outside linebacker, and miss.

Assuming what the defender will do rather than making the read.

COACHING POINTS
Key is taking the defender where he wants to go.

Eyes inside when going up field.

Steal Block

Our goal on this block is to take the defender "where he wants to go" if we run into an OLB in space. If he attacks we can kick him out or reach him. We understand that we are outmatched in the speed department, and do not want to hold.

If the force player disappears - which can happen due to us running a screen often in this concept, we would then get our eyes inside for the ILB or any player responsible for force in the defensive scheme. The same premise would be true - try to seal them, but take them where they "want to go". Just do not hold.

This type of block is also worked on during our "blocking in space" POD.

Chute Drills

Chute Drills

While many schools will use the chute more often, we have found using bodies for blocking has been better for our athletes. We will use "cues" such as a bad or a hand to keep our pad level low.

However, we will use these chute drills, especially early in the season to focus on staying low off the ball. Here are our base drills we prefer from the chutes:

Chute Drills
- Sprint
- Short & Choppy
- Pulls (Right and Left)

Chute drills are a great way to train your players at staying low.

Mix up the hand that is down and which foot the player is stepping with first.

We have found it works better to start inside the chute.

Always go on a cadence.

For drill videos follow the QR code:

Chute Drills - Stance

ALL LINEMEN

PURPOSE
Teaching lineman how to play low, while still playing fast.

KEY SKILLS
Balance
Low pad level

SETUP
Chute is needed, if no chute is available you can also line up a few hurdles.

DRILL INSTRUCTIONS
(2) Different Drills
- Sprint Thru
- Pulls

For each you will start inside the chute. Mix up which hand is down.

Always go on a cadence.

COMMON MISTAKES
Hands are not in proper place.

Up on toes, when doing short and choppy drill.

COACHING POINTS
We utilize the chute drills during our warmups. Most do them often enough to where the players will be trained at staying low.

Chute Drills

Sprints
- For this the players will sprint thru the chute.
- The purpose of the drill is to play low and fast.
- Hand placement does not matter for this drill. Only going as fast as possible while stay low.

*We can also set this drill up for a down block similar to what we have shown in that section, by having our player start at the end of the chute and step for a down block.

Chute Drills

Pulls (Right and Left)
- The purpose of this chute drill is teaching staying low on your first two steps of your pull.
- Be sure to do it each way and mix up the hand that is the ground.
- Start inside the chute.

Chute Drill Overview

- Chute drills are an excellent way to train players on the proper height to block.

- You can add to this depending on what type of chutes you have. If yours is an open chute you can marry it very easily with down block drills.

Chute Drills

Goal of the chutes

Our entire goal of working with a chute is to teach a low takeoff. While we are not a pure Wing-T system, we do want to establish a low pad level.

We can run many of these same drills with our "buck hurdles" as the season progresses.

POD Drills

POD DRILLS

These are drills that need to be worked with and for specific spots on our line. It is a skill that a specific position in our offense needs to be able to execute. While it would not be "wrong" to do this with all linemen, it would be wasted time as we never as those positions to perform these blocks.

In this section you will find POD's for our guards, quick side of the line, center/guards, guards/tackles, guards and tight-ends and more. We basically want to work positions that will perform these types of blocks together.

This would include:
Double Team Drills – While we rep these with all players, we want to focus on those who work together.

Pull Drills – Often our Guards and Tight-ends.

Screen Drills – One side of the line or the middle of the line.

HURDLE DRILL
Guards and Y's

PURPOSE
Working on blocking on pulls.

This is used in Buck, Belly and Counter.

DRILL INSTRUCTIONS
We will move the hurdles to simulate kickout blocks and wrap blocks. This drill will be used in multiple ways.

The goal is to work footwork for pulling.

Often we will include our backfield action.

COMMON MISTAKES
Slowing down at hurdle

Not running as fast as possible.

COACHING POINTS
We want to run "through the block" so we use the hurdles.

Angle the hurdles to cause the wrapping guard to get his "eyes inside".

We will often move the kick hurdle up-field to simulate coming "downhill" on kick blocks.

KEY SKILLS
Learning angles and how to explode through blocks.

We want the wrapping guard to gain depth on his 2-4th steps and then square to the line.

SETUP
We like oversized Hurdles, but this drill can be done with cones/dummies.

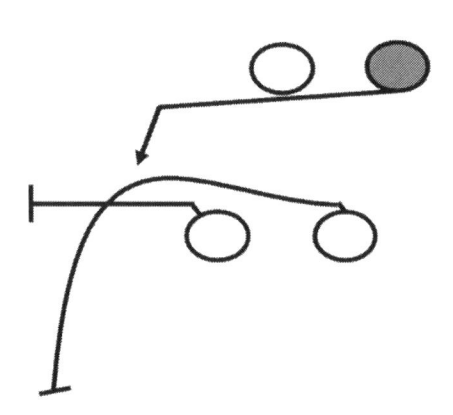

Hurdle Drill

A picture of our "Hurdle" drill. We will often add in hurdles for our linemen to work on coming out of their stance low. Notice in this picture the 4' hurdle that is next to our Quick Guard to cause him to come out of his stance low.

We also will angle the hurdles slightly to cause our linemen to run at the correct angle. The "kick" hurdle is angled out to cause our guard to work on "rooting out" the defensive player and the "pull" hurdle is angled inside to cause our guard to get his eyes and body angled to pick up an inside player.

Hurdle Drill

The next progression from the hurdle drill is to remove the hurdles. Now we will use coaches or scout players to represent the defense.

We do this to get more of a moving target and game-like look for our guards. They run through the correct hip of the coach and we can simulate pressure from different areas.

Hurdle Drill

As we advance our "hurdle" drill to coaches, we like to use a hand slap on the correct shoulder of the coach to simulate our aiming points. In the above picture the guard on the right is working his aiming point for a "kick-out" block as the wrapping guard is reading the ILB to see which shoulder to attack.

In our offense we attempt to block a ½ a man. The reason we do this, is often our guards are outweighed by all LB's.

Hurdle Drill

This is the goal for our wrapping guard. Notice how he has his eyes "inside" looking for pursuit. He will naturally want to "chase" defenders and we do not want this. We want him to run his track and the running back will cut off of him. We also NEVER WANT TO SLOW DOWN. This is why we use the hurdles and progress up.

Spacial Blocking

Quick Side of Line and Center

PURPOSE

Working blocks for screen game or 2nd level down blocks. Blocks that require us to "come to balance".

DRILL INSTRUCTIONS

We will begin with cones and progress to people.

We want linemen to work to release down field and settle at a "hip" of the player.

The "hip" represents the leverage we want them to keep.

COMMON MISTAKES

Do not come to balance

Work at wrong angles – go where the defense will be not where they are.

.

COACHING POINTS

We will set this drill up in multiple ways to simulate plays/blocks.

The main point is to get feet moving and come to balance.

KEY SKILLS

Quick Feet

Great Balance

SETUP

In the set-up below we have a screen drill.

We will also do this with downblocking at the 2nd level.

Often we will take the quick tackle and only work him with the WR's on screen drills.

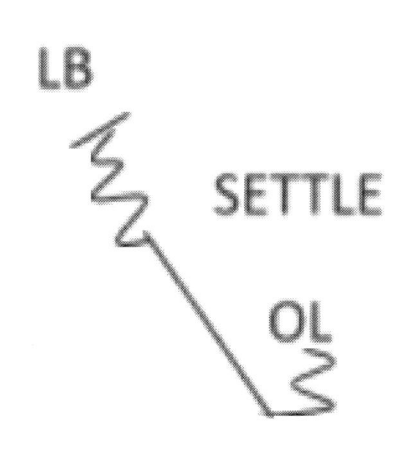

Blocking in Space

Blocking in space is key for most of our linemen (with the main exception being our Strong Tackle. We do work different types of blocking in space depending on the position.

The main screens we run are to the quick side or middle of the field. So, we often work our Quick Side of the line, with a coach/cones as this block does require them to settle in space. We will also work with our interior linemen for our middle screen.

While we are working this drill, we are often working the other linemen on pass protection or a block they need improvement on.

Blocking in Space

Blocking in space is difficult for linemen. We usually take them with our WR's or at least our WR coach to teach them how to understand angles and how to settle our feet.

In this picture #3 is doing a great job of coming to balance and will take the defender wherever he chooses to go on this fast screen. #22 is working his leverage on the linebacker and forcing him to commit to coming under or over the block and then he will engage.

Most of the work on blocking in space is effort and coming to balance for our linemen. Allowing them to work with a coach that understands that will help tremendously.

Settle Drill

ALL SKILL

PURPOSE

Teaching our players to come under balance and control

How to use hands and feet without holding

DRILL INSTRUCTIONS

We will begin with little space and work this drill to gradually increase the space the player must cover

Player must sprint off the ball and then come under balance and mirror the defender while striking with his hands

COMMON MISTAKES

Players will overrun the block and not settle

Players will lunge after a block or reach with hands

Players will not close the space and give too much room for the DB to elude the block

COACHING POINTS

Fire off the ball to make them think it could be a route

Settle with "hot" feet.

Elbows in as we punch

KEY SKILLS

Learning to block in space

SETUP

Can be done in any space

Prefer to start them at 5 yards and work up

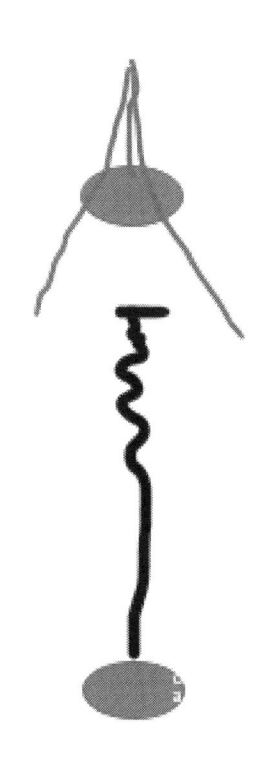

Coach: Gives direction when and where to come up field

105

Settle Drill

Usually this drill is run by our Wide Receiver Coach, as he has more experience with this type of block. We will put whichever linemen - generally the Quick Tackle and Quick Guard (and potentially the Strong Guard) - in with the WR group and allow them to work this drill.

It is helpful for them to see the block performed in space and understand how we must come to balance on these types of blocks.

This type of block is common for us with our Quick Tackle on "steal" calls and in our screen game.

We want to be "come to balance" as we approach a defensive player.

Counter POD Drill
SG and Y

PURPOSE
Working TE/G's on pull kick and wrap drill for our Counter Play.

Can be used for other pull drills.

KEY SKILLS
Working on angle of kick and the angle of the wrap.

We want to gain depth with TE as he pulls to wrap.

SETUP
Often done with our over-sized hudles or with coaches/bags.

Done on a line to work depth of pulls.

DRILL INSTRUCTIONS
We like to do this with the backfield action so we can work angles and timing for counter.

Will often use hurdles/dummies early in the season to give angles.

COMMON MISTAKES
Pull Kick – slows down or takes on with wrong shoulder

Pull Wrap – does not get enough depth on pull or get his eyes back inside.

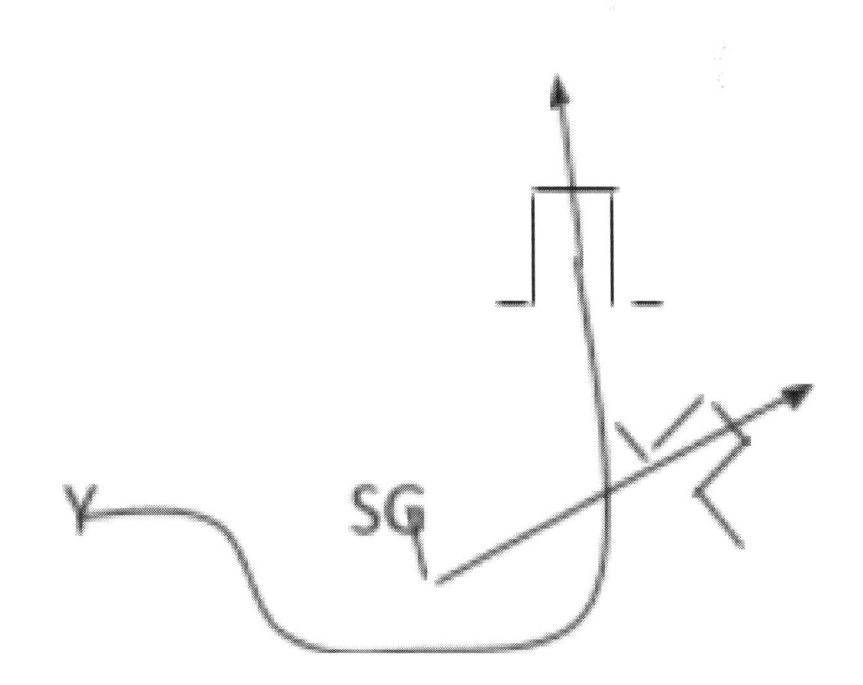

COACHING POINTS
We want to "rip the lanwmower" as we pull.

TE should gain depth on steps 2-4 and then get square. He almost runs a "U" shape to get his eyes inside.

POD for Counter

This drill is common for us to start off with using the hurdles we do on our Buck Drill. As we progress, we like to have coaches/scout players representing defenders. We teach this the same as our buck sweep drill.

This drill was on a Thursday practice before we started our quick practice, thus no hurdles or coaches.

We will rotate through all of our guards and tight-ends as well as the backfield portion.

Trojan Pod
Guards and F's

PURPOSE

Working on reading the block for Trojan.

Also, working to teach our linemen to get their eyes inside.

DRILL INSTRUCTIONS

We will use either another lineman or coach as the "wing".

The goal is the first puller reads this block and the second follows.

Can easily be run right after our "buck" pod time.

COMMON MISTAKES

Not enough depth on first puller to read the block.

Eyes not inside.

COACHING POINTS

Get depth on first few steps and width.

Eyes inside once we decide on a course of action.

All other pullers follow the first puller…even if he was wrong on his read.

KEY SKILLS

Learning to read the block of the wing.

Learning to get our eyes inside and wrap tight off the blocks.

SETUP

Often can be done with "buck pod".

May want to use other potential pulling linemen. .

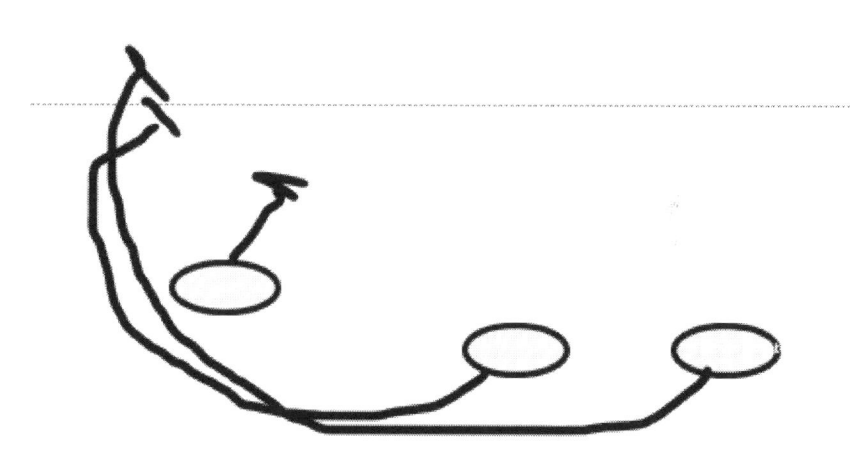

Trojan POD

Here is the progression of our POD.

Picture one shows the set-up. We are reading the block of the "off-guard" as he will either seal or kick the defensive end. We feel by working at this spot the guards begin to understand how that block happens.

Picture two shows that the block turned into a reach and the first puller should be reading this block.

Picture three shows both guards wrapping with their eyes going inside for the filling LB/DB's.

Trojan POD

Here are some examples of the guard reading the block of our wing in a game. The wing has sealed the defender inside, and the first puller must wrap outside of the seal block, while keeping his eyes inside for the first threat coming from the inside.

Common issues you will face with this type of block:
1) Linemen don't read the block of the wing correctly
2) Linemen keep eyes too wide which causes them to pull to wide and miss inside defenders

The design of the play has the "B" blocking the force player. If he is hooked, there should be NO defender outside of him that we are accounting for with our guards. It is important for them to understand that all their threats to make a tackle are inside.

Double Teams

DOUBLE TEAM
ALL LINEMEN

PURPOSE

Working on coming off to LB

We want to teach how to communicate as we work to 2nd level.

KEY SKILLS

Keeping contact 1st level defenders.

We want to post and knock

Usually our inside player will "post" with his outside hand and keep eyes on LB

Our knock player will "knock" them inside with his shoulder as he keeps his eyes on the 2nd level defender.

SETUP

We will use a scout player at the first level and another playing at LB depth.

Coach will point to where he wants the LB to "fit".

We will also move our DL in other places.

DRILL INSTRUCTIONS

The goal is to give multiple looks in this drill.

We will move our DL from a shade, to head up.

Also, want our LB to fit over the top or fit inside.

COMMON MISTAKES

Both linemen leave DL and do not get push.

OL does not see second level defenders and drop their head..

COACHING POINTS

We want to have our hands and no space between our OL.

We want to "Post and knock".

One Linemen gets vertical push and the other wants to knock him and seal him horizontally.

Post-Knock

In our offense this is how we prefer to teach the double team. The goal for us is the inside player is the "seal" and the outside is the "knock" as they work onto the 2nd level block. The pictures below show the progression with our Strong Tackle and Center on a 1-Technique on Buck.

Post-Knock

Here is a good example of a post-knock in a game. In this example we are double teaming with a guard (player on the right in the picture) and tackle (player on the left in the picture.

The tackle's job is to "knock" the defensive lineman as he moves on to the linebacker. The guard's job is to "overtake' the defensive lineman and seal him inside.

The only adjustment we would like to see from the tackle, is for him to be more "square" to the line so that he can move on to the next level better.

Pass Protection

PASS PROTECTION
ALL LINEMEN

PURPOSE

Working on Picking up blitzers in pass protection.

We teach a vertical set, protecting inside gap first and passing off to outside.

KEY SKILLS

Balance

Communication

Footwork

SETUP

Run with partnered groups of 2.

Coach will stand behind and direct stunts and areas he wants the scout defense to move.

DRILL INSTRUCTIONS

We will attempt to do this drill with partners and two scout players to simulate 2nd level pass rush.

The coach stands behind and tells the stunt to the scout players.

OL will pass set and communicate the stunt while protecting the inside.

COMMON MISTAKES

Linemen will lunge at defenders instead of maintain balance.

No communication on Blitzing.

Turn shoulders out and allow inside rush.

COACHING POINTS

Keep Shoulders Square

Communicate

Punch first level defender, but keep eyes on second level defender

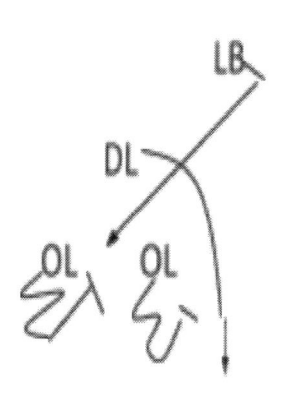

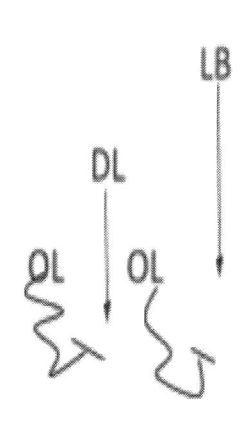

We will also work this and not blitz the LB.

Or we can work this with 2 DL that will twist.

The goal is force communication and balance with our offensive line.

Roll Out Pass Protection
Lineman and Backs

PURPOSE
Working rollout protections.

KEY SKILLS
Keeping balance
Communicating all stunts

SETUP
We do this with full line during group work. Can be done on air or vs a defense.

DRILL INSTRUCTIONS

Playside lineman will stay flat. Backside lineman will be flat for two steps and then hinge.

Once engaged with a defender, that's your guy.

COMMON MISTAKES

Players will disengage from our blocks or not maintain good footwork

Players will come off their path (playside) and not see blitzing LB's

Backside Players will not get depth if their gap is not attacked

COACHING POINTS

Center will always stay flat with the play side.

Roll Out

We keep our roll out protection simple for our players. We will work to the gap-over. If we lock onto a player, we do not let go.

If we are playside: If nobody shows we will look for LB and then engage inside gap.

If we are backside: If nobody shows, we would gain depth and hinge for rushers off the backside.

Roll Out

This is an example of working our players on roll out with the coach giving a different look from the defense.

Once we teach our base rules, our next goal is to give different looks to the offensive line to see what may show up in a game.

Common mistakes we see -

1) Players will disengage from our blocks or not maintain good footwork
2) Players will come off their path (playside) and not see blitzing LB's
3) Backside Players will not get depth if their gap is not attacked

Roll Out

This is an example of our roll out protection in a game. It is not perfect, but will help a coach understand the concept. This would be "rodeo" or roll out to the right. Our linemen will attack the first player on the right. The play side will then peel back inside if no pressure shows up.

Conclusion

It is our hope that you were able to find some tips in each drill. While they are geared for the Gun T, these drills can be run in most gap-scheme offenses. It is my belief that as the offensive line goes, so goes the offense.

This position is the most difficult to coach in all of football, as a coach must not only provide the knowledge, but also the motivation to get a group to function as one. Be sure to push and coach your position, but also make sure they know you care about them. We work to reward our players as often as possible. Between pancake dinners and lineman of the week awards, we want to them to recognize their importance.

A team will only succeed if their line is giving 100% effort with the right technique. We feel we create great effort, by showing our linemen how they can be successful.

While each year we always look for drills that can fit our system, this book contains the drills we feel are most important. Running these drills within the Gun T System will ensure that your linemen are prepared.

About the Authors

Kenny Simpson is a football coach in Arkansas and the creator of the [Gun T RPO Offensive System](#).

With experience as a Head Coach at three different schools, Coach Simpson has learned what it takes to transform a program into a winning organization. Taking over a program that had won eight games in five seasons and had been on a 20-plus game losing streak, Coach Simpson led Southside Charter High School to the playoffs for four-consecutive seasons and won two conference titles. For his efforts, he was named 4A-2 Conference Coach of the Year (2017), a finalist for Hooten's Coach of the Year (2017) and was the All-Star Nominee for the 4A-2 (2016 and 2019).

He is married to Jamey and has three children: Avery, Braden and Bennett. The couple was married in 2001 after meeting at Harding University.

Bo Gould is the offensive line coach at Southside Charter in Batesville, Arkansas. He also serves many other roles at Southside including Head Softball Coach.

He is married to Amber and they have six children. (Emilee, Tyler, Lane, Rylee, Kaylee, and Maddox)

Made in the USA
Middletown, DE
01 May 2025